Poetry from the Soul... for the Soul

Volume II

Adrienne Thompson

Pink Cashmere Publishing

Arkansas, USA

ISBN: 0-9971461-1-7

ISBN-13: 978-0-9971461-1-0

Dear Reader,

I can't thank you enough for purchasing this book of poetry. It is near and dear to my heart as I have been a poet for most of my life. Long before I ever considered penning a novel, I wrote poetry to express myself. It has always been a way for me to cope with life's ups and downs, and it is not easy for me to share my innermost thoughts and feelings with the public. Nevertheless, here I am doing just that. It is my hope that this short collection of poetry blesses you in some way, shape, or form.

It is arranged in the order in which it was written—from oldest to newest. I believe this arrangement gives it a more organic feel. I truly hope you enjoy reading it!

Blessings,

Adrienne Thompson

"I can do all things through Christ who strengthens me."

Philippians 4:13 (NKJ

Happiness

Happiness came slowly

Long after childhood

Where worries often stifled my smile

Long after puberty

When hormones overshadowed joy

Not during adolescence

When I was too concerned with the future

Way after coming of age

When so many mistakes were made

But in the Middle Ages

When I came to know myself

When the reflection in the mirror shifted

Did I learn to smile

And came to realize that circumstances

And concerns

And truths

And lies

Have nothing to do with happiness

Walls

I spent most of my life building up walls to hide behind

Cloistered from a world I longed to live in

Drilling tiny holes here and there

Peeking out at the people

Watching as their lives passed me by

I longed for a life of my own

But fear paralyzed me

Rejection taunted me

Saying that it would always be there

I placed a ladder at the wall

Climbed to the top and peered down at the people

Heard their laughter

Saw their smiles

My heart ached

My head swelled with possibilities

I wanted a friend

I needed a lover

It was time to live…

It was time to live

So with a swift kick

And the force of my will

I knocked down my walls

And walked into the sunlight

Its warmth was so comforting

Its rays so inviting

It was nice to walk amongst the living

I turned my back on my walls

And in that moment

I began to live

Black Onyx

I wish my skin shone like the night

Like the dark sky, devoid of stars

I wish my blackness was like that of my ancestors

I wish my regality was like that of black onyx,

Rare and coveted by the treasure hunters of the world

Like the sands of Kaimu Beach

Like the pupils of my children's eyes

I wish for the comfort of my grandmother's ebony skin

For the reassurance of her kinky hair

I miss the thickness of her lips, the strength of her loving arms

I pray for the pride that was once so characteristic of my people

I pray for the community that is slowly fading away

Bring back my blackness in all its glory

Bring back my blackness

Grateful

Aware

Awake

Being

Breathing

Feeling

Seeing

Tasting

Knowing

Loving

Walking

Running

Climbing

Sitting

Doing

Grateful

Peace in my Piece

A soft wind caressing my skin

The warmth of a lover's embrace

A gentle caress, a smile on my face

Not rushing, but moving at my own pace

Dancing in the rain

Not caring what others think

No longer hiding my pain

Shedding the thick skin that walled me in

Jamming out to a song

Singing loudly and off-key

Smiling for no reason at all

Imagining him and me

Living in the realm of possibility

Blocking out the negativity

Shrugging when people stare at me

Today I choose to live

And to find peace in my piece

He

He loves her with his whole heart

With every fiber of his being

Would die for her

Would lie for her

He's hopelessly devoted to her

He lives her

Wakes up in the morning for her

Is blessed by her existence

If he were to lose her

His heart would not mend

For her, he breathes

With her, life begins and ends

She is his muse

His life source

Her love nourishes him

He loves her

Undeniably so

He loves her

Addicted To Pain

I think I might be addicted to pain

Because without it I just don't feel the same

Maybe my childhood is to blame

For my addiction to pain

I feel lost without that sting

Have no stories to bring

The hurt makes my head ring

And gives me a song to sing

Disappointment is the fuel

That powers my muse

It's the sorrow I often use

The misery gives me clues

My heart is connected to the clouds

The thunder brings me out

The lightening illuminates my path

I see beauty in nature's wrath

A tear can spark an idea

Heartache brings success near

Harsh words I often hear

To me can be so dear

Am I out of my mind

That in sadness I find

Motivation to climb

The pinnacle of my creative mind?

I'm addicted to pain

It finds me in my hiding place

Takes me to a darker space

A place where I can create

I'm addicted to pain.

This Man

He smiles, makes me blush

Says one word, makes my blood rush

Blinks his eyes and to my surprise

I feel a love for him that sends me high

He laughs or frowns, in his eyes I seem to drown

His skin, his scent, his hair—they take me there

This man that God made for me

His heart, it calls me

His touch, his warmth, are all I need

This man, this man that God made for me

JAZZ!

I hear the horns, the glorious horns, as the tune begins to build

The drums, the cymbals, they drive the beat, they turn the wheel

The piano, ebony and ivory—what a magical melody they make

The bass, the bottom, where the foundation is placed

Play it, boys!

That jazz I like

It tickles my poor soul

Play it! Play it, boys!

I wanna dance inside my soul

Play those horns of silver and gold

Make me smile, send my heart back to yesterday

I wanna dance the night away

GREATNESS

Is it wrong to see greatness in myself?

To know that a power rests in my soul?

Is it wrong to desire to be nothing less than a queen who sits upon a throne?

Is it wrong to hold my head up high, to know my worth, to understand the what, when, and why?

To fully know who I am and *whose* I am?

Is it wrong to think and contemplate, to ponder and hypothesize?

Should I pretend to be less?

Should I shrink and fade away?

Or should I open my mouth, share my thoughts, and put my greatness on display?

ONE LESS COW

No, sir

Not I

Not today

You wanna play?

Well, first you gotta pay

Not with dollars and cents or plastic credit

Not with diamonds and gifts or cars or debit

But with respect and love and fidelity must you tender

On bended knee, a ring as your fee, with your heart you must render

A contract of sorts between you and me

Together we shall become one

Then and only then, my dear sir, can you have your fun

Many a cow is used, her milk drained without thought

But one less cow you'll find in me

Only through marriage can my virtue be bought

A Dreamer

Sometimes I close my eyes and pretend that what I see is real

That what I know is true

That what I want is mine

What an imagination I must have

To hold these fantasies so close to my heart

To see the impossible as possible

To expect what can never be to be

A dreamer at heart I am

A lover of love, never to have it be mine

What a dreamer I am

What a dreamer I am…

They tried it...

They tried to smother me with black cotton

Tried to strangle me with beige intentions

Tried to stab me with the keys to my own freedom

Tried to shoot me with the gun of their expectations

Tried to bind me with their stereotypes

Tried to hide me behind failed equality

Tried to pacify me with a check or two

Tried to fool me about who's zooming who

Tried to lie me into submission

Tried to bully me into supposition

Tried to convince me they were right

Tried to make me believe white = the highest height

Tired

I'm tired of the racists hating
And the privileged ones berating
And the media creating
An atmosphere for the hating

I'm tired of the lying
And the people who are trying
Being pushed down when vying
To keep from dying

I'm tired of being told I'm crazy
For thinking I'm amazing
The societal hazing
The leeches are feeding and grazing

I'm tired of waiting
And hoping that maybe
They'll see and stop debating

About why they keep hating

I'm tired of shouting loud

And proving that I'm proud

And getting lost in the crowd

While to succeed I'm disallowed

I'm fed up with the lies

Tired of the rise

In people whose lives

Are not counted as a prize

But more than that

I'm tired of the false white hat

And the idle chit-chat

As my people are swatted away like gnats

Yeah, I'm tired of that

Single Motherhood

Heartbreak

Heartache

Pain

Shame

Grief

Fear

Tears

Progress

Set backs

Trying

Working

Loving

Failing

Succeeding

Hidden despair

A brave front

Taking care

Neglecting self

Worrying

Hoping

Praying

Doing

Molding

Faking

Deciding

Thinking

Missing sleep

Stumbling

Standing tall

Losing

Winning

Mission accomplished

Empty nest

Loneliness

FAMILY

Family

At times

Makes me wonder

If I'm

Losing my

Young mind

Over

Once upon a time

Very long ago

Egos collided

Ruining what we had

Hope

Helps me make it

Over the hump of despair

Provides a bridge for me to

Eternity

Hate

Hate never solved anything

Actions speak louder than words

To love is to be human

Even when we're flawed

Remembering

I remember him

How could I forget?

I loved him strong

Unconditionally, I accepted his flaws

I believed every word he spoke

I trusted his heart

Fused mine with it

Looked forward to a life with him

I thought he was the one

Thought I was made for him

Believed our souls had found one another

Prayed we'd always be together

Evidently I'm a fool

Or I was

And blind

And deaf

He didn't love me

Couldn't love me

Broke me down

Shattered my soul

But I let him

I watched him ruin me

Cried but wouldn't leave

Tried to make it work

But it couldn't

It wasn't real love

I don't even think he liked me

How could he when I didn't even like myself?

He used me

Almost used me up

Almost ground me to dust

Almost erased me

But I let him
So what does that say about me?
Or my self-esteem?

He made a fool of me
But I let him

For years I mourned
What we had
A one-sided love affair

I missed him
As he moved on
To woman after woman
I stood still

He dragged me down to the gutter
And left me there

But I let him

So what does that say about me?

He Say

He say he like my smile

The way I laugh

My sense of style

He say that when I walk

My hips have him grinnin'

He love the way they talk

He say he love my mind

The way I think

How I be trippin' sometimes

He say he love my lips

And when he kiss me

It make his heart skip

He say I'm the bomb

He don't wanna lose me

'Cause I'm his lucky charm

He say we so in tune

He gon' marry me

We gon' have a wedding next June

He say we soul mates

And that he love me the most

That's what he say

Gossip

Girl, no!

You playing!

You're kidding!

When?

Last night?

No, she didn't!

Not with him?

Again?

Well, what'd he say?

You lying!

Girl, for real?

Was he spying?

Then what?

No!

Shut your mouth!

Dang, girl. I gotta go.

Call me back

I wanna hear more

I know, chile

But someone's at the door

Yeah, I will

Oh, I see

Yeah, about five

Okay then, goodbye

Hey, girl... come on in

No, not busy at all

On the phone

Talking to Tina again

Come on in, girl

Have a seat

Guess what she told me about Betty

Honey, you are in for a treat!

Come on

Come on

Enough talking

Enough contemplating

Enough stalking

We done discussed it enough

Laid down the ground rules

I know what you like

I know what makes you drool

I'm willing and ready

Alone and waiting

I just want what I want

I'm tired of all this dating

So bring it on

If you're feeling what I'm feeling

Cause I'm digging you, boy

And the suspense is killing

Honesty

If I am honest with you, I'll tell you the truth
I'll tell you that the thought of you scares me

If I am honest with you, I'll not hide my face
I'll show you the fear in my eyes

I'll let you feel my apprehension
Tell you all about my past

I'll be up front and come clean
About the man who hurt me last

I'll tell you that what you represent
Scares me to death

I'll tell you that if you kiss me, touch me
I'll hold my breath

I'll tell you that I don't trust men

Stopped believing in them long ago

I'll tell you that you don't stand a chance

That you might as well just go

But if you decide to stay

And tough it out

If you decide it's worth the effort

To wait me out

If you grab your hammer

And knock down my walls

Maybe I'll tell you

That I love you after all

Paid in Full

I am not worthy
Neither are you
But still He gave His life
Made all things new

I am a sinner
Not worth a thin dime
But still He hung His head
And for me, He died

I make mistakes daily
Not perfect by a longshot
But still He saw my potential
And my old soul He bought

I am nothing to speak of
Just dust, here and then gone
But He loved me still

And with His life, forgiveness is sown

He paid it all for me
Undeserving little me
Imperfect as I may be
He paid it all for me

Faith

Forging on

And believing for the best

In spite of darkness

Taking Him at His word

Handing Him the reins

Haiku for Christopher

Precious little boy

Made my life so much richer

With just your sweet smile

Haiku for Olivia

Though you're not born yet

I know that I will love you

With all of my heart

The Cycle

I sin

I cry

I travail

I repent

Then I sin again

My heart is willing

My flesh is oh so weak

But by God's grace

I am still here

He keeps giving me chances

To get it right

Imperfect

I ain't perfect

Ain't wrapped in cellophane

Ain't spit shined and glossed up

Ain't no glitter on me

Ain't no applause when I enter the room

Ain't no makeup that'll help

Ain't no diets that'll fix it

Ain't no high fashion that'll mask it

Ain't no fake smile that'll force it

I ain't perfect

And that's all right with me

Saved

HE didn't have to do it

Send HIS only son

HE didn't have to save me

HE didn't have to care

HE didn't have to rescue me

Snatch me from the grave

HE didn't have to weep for me

HE didn't have to love me

But I'm glad HE did

Just one

One plate

One cup

One pillow

One toothbrush

One voice

One body

Single

Love

Looking for you

Optimistic that I'll find you

Vying for your attention

Ever alone

Stupid

Saw him

Tried to talk to him

Used to know him

Played the game with him

In time, was hurt by him

Died inside because of him

A haiku for me

Daughter, wife, mother

Divorced, still a mother, alone

Nurse, writer, dreamer

Remembering again

It was in the middle of July the first time he lied to me

I remember it was hot, sticky

Unbearable

Or maybe it was June

And summer had just stuck its head in the door and
waved a bit of heat into the room

Promising to stay for a long visit

It could've been May, though

I don't know

But he lied

I should've ended things right then

I should've back-peddled

I should've saved myself some grief

But instead I said

What's one lie?

What could it hurt?

It hurt me

My heart

The first blow

The first ache

And it all began in July

Or June

Or May

With one lie

The Struggle

It's crazy when you're broke

The things that'll pop into your head

The ideas you get

That are better left unsaid

The lengths to which you'll go

To get your kids fed

The nights you toss and turn

While lying in your bed

The sacrifices you make

Watching them eat instead

Of you who sit there with an aching head

Satisfied that they'll have sweet dreams with their hunger shed

It's amazing the decisions you have to make

The bills you pay late

The enormous crippling weight

Of having poverty as your fate

No one wants this life
And truly it ain't right
To flip the switch and see no light
It's a hard battle to fight

But in the midst of despair
Hope lingers there
From friends who share
From people who care

They lend a helping hand
For they truly understand
That some of us women still have to stand
With no help from a man

We strive to thrive
We pray to stay alive
Hoping one day to arrive

Hoping our children do more than survive

I UNDERSTAND

I understand why the dope boy sells

Why the angry mother yells

Why the prostitute compels

Why that little girl is in a shell

Why that brother is in jail

Why that student won't excel

Why that sister rose and fell

Why she's still waiting to exhale

Why the hood is hell

Why the mailman dropped the mail

Why the city has that smell

Why some kids ignore the school bell

Why the rappers tell tales

Why your boat ain't got no sail

Why so many people fail

Why it's so hard for a black male

Why the church is leaving out details

Why the victims won't tell

Why the train jumped the rails

Why the doctors can't fix what ails

Why justice won't prevail

Why our protectors practice betrayal

Why the sighted need Braille

Why the food of thought is so stale

Why misery rains down like hail

Why he was innocent but couldn't make bail

Why Lady Justice dropped her scales

Why progress moves like a snail

Why freedom is so pale

And the rich continue to assail

And the poor still travail

And the lost still get email

It ain't right

But I understand it well

Free

Descended from slaves

Strong people, survivors

Worked their fingers to the bone

But still found time to love

Hopeful people

Believers

Strivers

They sought freedom

They dreamt of broken chains, in shackled feet

We are a dream come true

A hope realized

We are free

But we don't know it

never forget

the ships

the stench of the journey

the bodies stacked in cramped quarters

then tossed overboard

the lives lost

chains

shackles

lost lineage

bondage

whips

lashings

scars

pain

fear

laws

overseers

field niggers

pickaninnies

house slaves

wet nurses

animals

jumping the broom

love

loss

auctions

bucks

wenches

property

sold off

broken families

lynchings

rape

emancipation

share cropping

no education

poverty

not really free

never forget

Lost one

Fingertips touching

Parting ways

Racing heart

Backwards gaze

Deep sigh

In a daze

Emotions heightened

Walking a maze

Constantly asleep

Eagerly awake

Contradicting myself

Always late

Too much time

Missed the date

Missing him

Fighting fate

Untitled

Have one or two of my kisses

See what real love tastes like

Feel my heart

Beating for you

Know me

The real me

Inside

The hidden one

The one I can only share

With you

Hold me

Until I cry

Until I die

Be there

Just be

Just be

Be Like

He be like a cool breeze in July

When the heat plasters itself to my skin

Like an ice water bath in the middle of a heat wave

Like my face in the freezer

Like a cherry Popsicle

Like an ice cream sundae

Like a fan blowing directly on me

Like AC

Like a summer rain

That's what he be like

Insomnia

Eyes open in the darkness

Quiet stillness

Soft snores surrounding me

A full bladder

Warm covers

A soft bed

Mind racing

Tired

But not tired enough

Wide awake

The suit

He wore a suit

So handsome

He almost took my breath away

Had a white smile

Brown skin

He was tall

Slim

But that suit…

It fit him just right

Wore some nice shoes, too

Smelled like Heaven

Mixed with a little bit of hell

And that suit…

It was black

White shirt underneath

Gold tie

Gold cuff links

Hair neatly cut

Beard trimmed

Mustache, too

Nice lips

Honey, that suit!

It looked expensive

Made him synonymous with money

And the way he walked

Nothing but confidence

That suit, though...

That suit is what got me

Yeah, it's all because of that suit

Talk to Me

Sit down for a moment

And talk to me

Show me what you see

Share your point of view

Tell me what's important to you

 Maybe it'll be important to me, too

What are your wishes, hopes, and dreams?

What does happiness to you mean?

Bring me up to speed

Keep me abreast

Give me the whole truth

And nothing less

Think of me as your journal

Lock your thoughts inside my mind

Hide me under your pillow

For no one to find

You can trust me

Yes, truthfully

Not a single word will I breathe

If in me you believe

I wanna help you bear the weight

Be your sounding board

And when you're done

We'll take it to The Lord

I'm here for you

This day and the next

So don't hesitate

To call or to text

Count me as your friend

Real and true blue

And remember

Together, we'll make it through

Visit the Poetry Foundation here:

http://www.poetryfoundation.org/

For more information about Adrienne Thompson, visit:

http://adriennethompsonwrites.webs.com

Sign up for Adrienne's newsletter here:

http://eepurl.com/jnDmH

Follow Adrienne on Twitter!

https://twitter.com/A_H_Thompson

Like Adrienne on Facebook!

https://www.facebook.com/AdrienneThompsonWrites

Join Adrienne's Facebook group!!

https://www.facebook.com/groups/674088779363625/

Follow Adrienne on Pinterest!

http://www.pinterest.com/ahthompsn/

Connect with Adrienne on Goodreads!

https://www.goodreads.com/author/show/5051327.Adrienne_Thompson

Also by Adrienne Thompson

The *Bluesday* Series:

Bluesday

Lovely Blues

Blues In The Key Of B

Locked out of Heaven (Tomeka's Story – A Bluesday Continuation)

The *Been So Long* Series:

Rapture (A Been So Long Prequel)

If (Wasif's Story) A Been So Long Prequel

Been So Long

Little Sister (Cleo's Story—a companion novel to Been So Long)

Been So Long 2 (Body and Soul)

Been So Long III (Whatever It Takes)

SEPTEMBER (The Christina Dandridge Story—a Been So Long companion novel)

The *Your Love Is King* Series

Your Love Is King

Better

The *Ain't Nobody* Series

Sedução (Seduction)—an Ain't Nobody Prequel

Ain't Nobody

Stand-alone novels:

Home

See Me

When You've Been Blessed (Feels Like Heaven)

Summertime (A Novella)

Nonfiction Titles:

Just Between Us (Inspiring Stories by Women) –as a contributor

Seven Days of Change (A Flash Devotional)

All books are available at amazon.com, barnesandnoble.com, and kobobooks.com

Visit **http://adriennethompsonwrites.webs.com** to download *Poetry from the Soul… for the Soul, Volume I* For FREE.

www.ingramcontent.com/pod-product-compliance
Lightning Source LLC
Chambersburg PA
CBHW060157070426
42447CB00033B/2192